Empower Your Journey

Your Growth Your Way

Rosemarie R Williams

Breaking The Chains

Understanding and Overcoming Victim Mentality

ISBN: 9798332352195

Imprint: Independently published

For permissions or inquiries, please contact the author at rosemaries-page@outlook.com

Breaking The Chains

In "Breaking The Chains: Understanding and Overcoming Victim Mentality," Rosemarie Williams takes readers on a transformative journey from feelings of helplessness to empowered living. This compelling guide delves into the psychological roots of victim mentality, a pervasive mindset that can trap individuals in cycles of self-pity, blame, and perceived powerlessness.

With empathy and expertise, Rosemarie unpacks the complex factors that contribute to a victim mentality, including past traumas, societal influences, and cognitive distortions. Through relatable anecdotes, real-life case studies, and cutting-edge research, she illuminates how this mindset can subtly infiltrate various aspects of life—impacting relationships, career growth, and personal happiness.

"Breaking The Chains" is not just about understanding the problem; it is a call to action. Rosemarie provides practical, actionable strategies for readers to reclaim their power and transform their lives. From cognitive-behavioral techniques and mindfulness practices to resilience-building exercises and self-compassion methods, this book offers a comprehensive toolkit for breaking free from the confines of a victim mentality.

Whether you're struggling with feelings of defeat, or simply seeking to enhance your emotional well-being, "Breaking The Chains" provides the insights and encouragement needed to foster a mindset of strength, responsibility, and hope. Rosemarie empowers readers to take control of their narratives, embrace their inherent worth, and step into a future defined by possibility and resilience.

Discover the liberating power of change and embark on a path to personal freedom with "Breaking The Chains: Understanding and Overcoming Victim Mentality."

Empower Your Journey - Your Growth, Your Way.

Contact Information
Rosemarie R. Williams rosemariespage@outlook.com

Empower Your Journey Series

Vol 1: A Guide to Preventing Interference with Your Personal Growth

Vol 2: Procrastination: Understanding its Origins to Achieve Success

Vol 3: Breaking Boundaries: A Guide to Stepping Out of Your Comfort Zone

Vol 4: Empower Your Destiny: Unleashing The Potential Within-Success Is Up To You

Vol 5: Breaking The Chains: Understanding and Overcoming Victim Mentality

Vol 6: Beyond The Chains: You Broke the Chains now it's Time to Rise Above Them

The Evolution of Self

A Journey from Limitation to Liberation

Introduction
Breaking the Chains

In the complex web of our minds, there's a force that can quietly hold us back—something we often don't see but can deeply feel: the victim mentality. Breaking the Chains: Understanding and Overcoming Victim Mentality is here to guide you through understanding this mindset and, most importantly, help you break free from it. Think of this book as your personal roadmap, designed to help you navigate the challenging terrain of self-perception, resilience, and empowerment.

As you move through these pages, you'll uncover the roots of victim mentality, see how it shows up in your life, and learn how it impacts your relationships, career, and overall happiness. Each chapter is like a key, unlocking a new understanding that can help you break the invisible chains holding you back.

But this journey isn't just about learning—it's about doing. That's why, at the end of each chapter, you'll find a journal section where you can reflect on what you've learned and start applying it to your own life. These journals are a safe space for you to explore your thoughts, confront old patterns, and begin to make real changes.

So, let's take this journey together. We'll dive deep into real-life stories, practical advice, and exercises that will challenge you to rethink how you see yourself and the world around you. By the end, you'll have not just the knowledge, but the tools and confidence to transform your mindset and your life.

Welcome to Breaking the Chains. Let's get started on your path to a stronger, more empowered you.

In this introductory chapter, we begin the journey of breaking free from the invisible chains of victim mentality. These chains can bind us in ways we may not even realize, holding us back from living a life of empowerment, growth, and fulfillment. As we delve into understanding how these chains are formed and how they impact our lives, we'll also explore the first steps toward liberation. The path to freedom starts with awareness, and in the pages ahead, you'll gain the insights and tools needed to start breaking those chains.

Now, let's turn inward and reflect on how these themes resonate with you personally.

Your Journey

"I am beginning a journey of liberation and self-empowerment."

Reflect

What does "breaking the chains" mean to you in the context of your life?

How do you currently perceive the concept of victim mentality?

Discover

Reflect on a time when you felt bound by circumstances or emotions.

What held you back, and what would it take to break free?

____

____

____

____

____

____

____

____

____

____

____

____

Transform

Identify one area in your life where you feel stuck. Consider what "breaking the chains" would look like in this context.

Set a small, actionable goal to start loosening the grip of that limitation.

____

____

____

____

____

____

____

____

____

____

____

____

____

____

____

____

____

____

____

____

____

____

Freedom rarely bursts through the door in a single moment. More often, it slips in quietly — through awareness, through courage, through the small choices that begin to loosen what once held you. With every moment of awareness, a link in the chain gives way. This is where your journey begins — one conscious choice, one new belief, one action at a time.

Understanding Victim Mentality and Its Ripple Effects

Victim mentality, also known as a victim mindset, is a psychological term that describes a way of thinking in which individuals perceive themselves as victims of the actions or circumstances around them. People with a victim mentality tend to believe that external forces, rather than their own choices or actions, are responsible for their current situation. This mindset doesn't just shape thoughts, it also influences emotions, behavior, and relationships, creating a ripple effect that can limit personal growth and opportunity.

Key characteristics of victim mentality include:

Blaming Others: Individuals with a victim mentality often blame others for their problems or difficulties. They may not take responsibility for their own actions and instead attribute negative outcomes to external factors.

Lack of Personal Agency: People with a victim mindset may feel powerless or helpless, believing that they have little control over their lives. This perception can lead to passivity and a reluctance to take initiative.

Negative Outlook: A victim mentality is associated with a generally negative outlook on life. Life often appears tinted by pessimism. Opportunities for growth are overshadowed by a focus on obstacles and what could go wrong.

Resistance to Feedback: Constructive input may be seen as criticism or proof that the world is against them, rather than an opportunity to learn.

Self-Pity: Viewing oneself as a perpetual victim fuels a cycle of negative thoughts and emotions, offering short-term comfort but long-term stagnation.

Adopting a victim mentality can be subtle, slipping into your life in ways that seem almost justified. Yet these habits quietly restrict potential, weaken resilience, and cloud judgment. Recognizing them is the first step toward liberation.

This chapter marks the beginning of that journey. In the pages ahead, we'll unpack each of these traits and explore how deeply they shape perception and behavior. But awareness alone isn't enough. My goal is to equip you with practical tools and strategies to challenge these patterns, reclaim your sense of agency, and create meaningful change.

This isn't just about recognizing the traits of a victim mentality, it's about actively transforming them. As we move forward, each chapter will guide you toward greater self-awareness, resilience, and optimism.

Together, we'll examine the thoughts, emotions, and behaviors that keep you stuck and uncover practical ways to foster growth, empowerment, and lasting positive change.

Victim mentality is often deeply rooted in our thoughts, behaviors, and beliefs. In this chapter, we explored the psychological underpinnings of this mindset, helping you identify how it might be manifesting in your life. By understanding the origins and characteristics of victim mentality, we can begin to dismantle its hold on us. The first step toward change is awareness, and as you gain clarity, you'll be better equipped to challenge and overcome this mindset.

Take a few moments to pause, breathe, and reflect on what this chapter revealed to you. As you move forward, take some time to reflect on your own experiences with victim mentality and consider how these insights might apply to your life.

Your Journey

"I am not defined by my past. I have the power to change my narrative."

Reflect

What beliefs or thoughts do you hold that might align with a victim mentality?

How have these beliefs influenced your behavior or decision-making in the past?

Discover

Reflect on a situation where you felt like a victim.

How does your understanding of victim mentality shape your view of that experience now?

____

____

____

____

____

____

____

____

____

____

____

____

Transform

Identify one limiting belief you have about yourself. Challenge it by writing down evidence that disproves it.

Consider how these new insights might change your approach to a current challenge.

____

____

____

____

____

____

____

____

____

____

____

Transformation begins with awareness. The more you reflect, the more your story evolves into one of strength and self-leadership.

Breaking the Blame Game
Confronting the Tendency to Shift Responsibility

The Trap of Blame

In the landscape of victim mentality, one of the most revealing traits is the instinct to place blame on others or on circumstances instead of taking personal responsibility. Blame can soothe the ego for a moment, but it quietly builds walls around our growth. Those caught in this pattern often deflect accountability, convincing themselves that their struggles exist solely because of someone else's actions or life's unfairness.

The Cycle That Blocks Growth

While blame may offer temporary relief, it quickly becomes a trap that stalls growth and empowerment. Each time blame is projected outward, an opportunity for self-reflection is lost — and with it, the chance for transformation. Real freedom begins the moment we turn inward and ask, *"What part did I play in this?"* That single question, though often uncomfortable, is where true transformation begins to take root.

Unseen Chains
Mark's Journey into Awareness

"I don't know how this keeps happening." That was Mark's go-to line — at work, at home, anywhere things went sideways. If a project fell apart, it was because the team didn't communicate. If a friendship soured, it was because the other person "just didn't understand." The story always made sense in his head — and for a while, it protected him from having to look too closely at his own reflection.

But one afternoon changed everything.

It was during a big presentation at work — a project Mark had been leading for weeks. When the meeting ended in confusion and missed points, his first reaction was familiar: frustration. He blamed his colleagues for not preparing properly. He blamed the system for being broken. But when his manager asked him, gently, *"What could you have done differently?"* — something inside him cracked.

The room went quiet. For the first time, he didn't have an answer.

That question followed him home that night. He replayed the day, the project, the countless moments he'd distanced himself from responsibility. He realized that blaming others had become a reflex — one that kept him safe from discomfort but also trapped in stagnation. Every time he pointed outward, he gave away a little more of his own power.

Over the next few weeks, Mark made a quiet promise to himself: to pause before assigning blame. When something went wrong, he asked, *"What part did I play in this?"* It wasn't easy. The truth rarely is. But slowly, the tone of his inner dialogue began to change.

Instead of seeing setbacks as proof that life was unfair, he started viewing them as mirrors — reflecting lessons he hadn't wanted to face. The more he practiced self-awareness, the lighter he felt. His relationships began to shift too. Colleagues noticed his openness; friends said he seemed calmer, more grounded.

Mark's journey wasn't about guilt — it was about growth. He learned that taking ownership didn't mean taking all the blame; it meant reclaiming the power to change.

Looking back, he says, "The hardest part wasn't admitting I was stuck in a victim mindset. It was realizing how much I'd been missing by holding onto it."

Now, when life throws challenges his way, Mark no longer asks, *"Why me?"* but rather, *"What is this here to teach me?"* And with that single shift, he turned the story of powerlessness into one of possibility.

Breaking Free from Blaming Others
A Guide to Overcoming Victim Mentality

Blame often feels like protection, but it's really a form of self-betrayal. By shifting responsibility onto others, we reinforce our sense of powerlessness and prevent ourselves from making positive changes. Understanding this tendency is crucial to breaking free from it.

Taking ownership isn't about guilt or fault; it's about reclaiming your power to shape what happens next.

Here's how to start that shift:

1. Reflect Honestly

Take a step back and notice where blame tends to show up in your life. Are there patterns? Times when it's easier to point the finger than to pause and ask, "What part of this do I own?" Honest reflection opens the door to real growth.

2. Take Responsibility, Not Blame

Owning your actions doesn't mean beating yourself up. It means saying, "I have influence here." Responsibility is strength — it's the moment you move from powerless to powerful.

3. Catch Negative Thought Patterns

Notice the stories that start with "It's not my fault." Challenge them. Ask yourself if there's another perspective — one that helps you move forward instead of staying stuck in frustration.

4. Be Open to Feedback

Feedback isn't a failure, it's information. The more open you are to hearing how others see things, the faster you grow. Listen with curiosity instead of defense; every insight is a mirror showing you what's ready to evolve.

5. Focus on Solutions, Not Faults

Instead of asking, "Who's to blame?" ask, "What can I do about it?" Break big problems into smaller pieces and take one small, intentional step at a time. Every solution you create builds confidence and momentum.

6. Practice Empathy

Try to see situations through someone else's eyes. Understanding where others come from softens judgment and helps you respond with compassion instead of blame.

7. Set Realistic Expectations

Unrealistic goals can fuel frustration. Start where you are, set achievable milestones, and celebrate progress — not perfection. Growth is a process, not a race.

8. Lean on Supportive People

Surround yourself with people who encourage you to take ownership — not those who feed your frustration. Share your progress and challenges with those who remind you of your strength.

9. Practice Mindful Awareness

Blame often lives in reactivity. Mindfulness — through breathing, journaling, or reflection — gives you space to choose your response. You can't control everything, but you can control how you show up.

10. Seek Professional Guidance

If you find the cycle difficult to break, therapy or coaching can offer tools and insights to move forward with confidence and clarity.

Breaking free from blame doesn't happen overnight — it's a practice. Some days, you'll catch yourself mid-blame and choose differently. Other days, you might fall back into old habits. That's okay. Every time you pause, reflect, and redirect, you're strengthening your awareness and reclaiming your agency.

Growth is a gentle process. Give yourself grace as you learn to own your story. Celebrate every win — even the quiet ones — and remember that setbacks aren't proof of failure. They're proof you're still learning.

Each choice to take responsibility rewrites your narrative. You stop living as the victim of circumstance and begin living as the author of your becoming. With every step, you create a life shaped by accountability, resilience, and truth — one that reflects the power you've had all along.

Take a moment now to reflect on how blame has played a role in your life and how you can begin to take responsibility for your own path forward.

Your Journey

"I choose to take responsibility for my life and my actions."

Reflect

How often do you find yourself blaming others for your circumstances?

What might happen if you took full responsibility for your life?

____

____

____

____

____

____

____

____

Discover

Reflect on a situation where you shifted blame to someone else.

How did this affect the outcome, and what would taking responsibility have looked like?

____

____

____

____

____

____

____

____

____

____

____

____

Transform

Identify one recent situation where you blamed someone else. Reframe it by considering your role in the outcome.

Practice taking responsibility in small, everyday situations to build the habit of ownership.

"I release the need to blame others and focus on my own growth."

Call to Action
Your Empowerment Journey Begins Now

You've seen how blame disempowers — now it's time to restore your strength through accountability.

Start Small: Take responsibility for one choice each day. Small actions create massive shifts.

Shift Your Focus: Regularly examine how you respond to challenges. Replace "Who's at fault?" with "What can I learn?"

Build Accountability Circles: Connect with people who remind you of your strength, not your excuses.

Seek Honest Voices: Invite feedback that challenges you to grow.

Stay Present: Awareness turns reaction into choice.

Celebrate Progress: Every step toward ownership is a victory of the spirit.

You hold the pen to your story. Each decision to take responsibility adds a new line of empowerment. Embrace challenges as opportunities to rise stronger, wiser, and freer. The moment you stop pointing fingers and start extending your hand toward growth your transformation begins.

As you embark on this transformative journey, view challenges as stepping stones to self-discovery and opportunities for honing your inner strength. Embrace the lessons they offer and allow them to mold you into a more resilient version of yourself. In the realm of personal responsibility, you become the architect of your destiny, crafting a narrative that reflects your values, aspirations, and unwavering commitment to growth.

Trust in your ability to navigate this path, for every stride forward is a testament to your strength and determination. The future is yours to shape, and as you step into this empowered mindset, you open the door to a world of endless possibilities and a life characterized by authenticity, purpose, and the fulfillment of your true potential.

Fostering Change
Steering Your Life With Intention

There comes a time when drifting through life no longer feels like peace — it feels like surrender. You watch opportunities pass, excuses pile up, and the same patterns repeat. You tell yourself, "It's just the way things are," but deep down, you know it isn't. That quiet ache inside is your spirit reminding you that you were never meant to be a bystander in your own story.

In the realm of a victim mindset, personal agency often fades behind the illusion of powerlessness. Those caught in this pattern believe life happens *to* them, not *through* them. This belief breeds helplessness and turns action into hesitation. Over time, initiative gives way to passivity, and the individual becomes a bystander in their own story.

When we hand over control of our lives to outside forces — circumstances, people, or luck — we unknowingly silence our own power. It's easy to blame what we can't control, but doing so keeps us in a constant state of reaction instead of creation. Life becomes something that happens *to* us, not something we actively shape.

Reclaiming your power begins with a single decision: to stop waiting for life to change and start becoming the one who changes it. Influence doesn't come from the outside — it starts within. Each thought, each response, each small choice is a stroke on the canvas of your destiny, shaping who you become and the life you build.

You are not at the mercy of life's current. You are the current — capable of shifting direction, creating movement, and carving your own path forward. The moment you choose to act instead of react, your story begins to change.

Lost in the Current
Sarah's Fight for Control

For years, Sarah moved through life like a passenger on a river she never chose. She'd tell herself she was just "going with the flow," but deep down, she knew the current had more say than she did. When a promotion slipped away or a relationship fizzled out, she shrugged and said, "It just wasn't meant to be." What she didn't realize was that each surrender chipped away at her sense of direction — until one day, she couldn't remember the last time she'd steered at all.

At work, she kept her ideas tucked neatly in the corners of her notebook. She'd listen as others shared suggestions she'd quietly thought of weeks before, forcing a smile while her stomach sank. *Maybe I'm not leadership material,* she told herself. *Maybe I'm meant to stay here.*

At home, decisions were left to others — where to eat, what to watch, even where to travel. It felt easier to say, "Whatever you want," than to risk disagreement. But each time she silenced her own preferences, she drifted a little farther from herself.

Then one morning, as she scrolled through her emails, she saw yet another congratulatory note — another promotion that had passed her by. Her chest tightened. She closed her laptop and stared out the window, realizing that the current she kept blaming for her direction was, in fact, her own silence.

Something shifted.

That afternoon, she set one small goal: speak up once in the next meeting. Her voice trembled when she finally did, but when her manager nodded and said, "That's a great point, Sarah," something inside her stirred — a spark she hadn't felt in years.

She began making small, deliberate choices: volunteering for a project, reconnecting with a friend she'd lost touch with, signing up for a class she'd always wanted to take. With each decision, the current slowed, and her hands found the oars again.

Through mindfulness and quiet reflection, Sarah learned to listen — not to fear or hesitation, but to the steady whisper of her own intuition. She started to see that control was never taken from her; she had simply stopped claiming it.

Now, when challenges come, she meets them with calm resolve. The current still flows — it always will — but she no longer drifts. She steers.

Sarah's story reminds us that freedom doesn't always begin with grand gestures. Sometimes, it starts with one quiet "yes" to yourself — the moment you stop floating and start guiding your own course.

Empowering Personal Agency
A Guide to Overcoming Victim Mentality

Growth begins when awareness meets action. The following steps are not rules — they're oars, helping you navigate your way back to center.

Cultivate Self-Awareness

Notice when feelings of helplessness arise. What triggers them? Awareness is the first spark that turns reaction into choice.

Challenge Limiting Beliefs

When you catch yourself thinking, *I can't change this,* pause. Ask yourself, *Is that true?* Replace self-defeating thoughts with affirmations that remind you of your strength.

Set Achievable Goals

Break ambitions into smaller, doable steps. Each completed task builds confidence and reinforces your influence over outcomes.

Take Consistent Action

Momentum grows from motion. Small, deliberate actions done consistently rewrite your inner story — one day, one choice, one moment at a time.

Own Your Choices: Acknowledge that you have the power to make choices, even in challenging situations. Accepting responsibility for your decisions empowers you to direct the course of your life. You can't control every outcome, but you can always choose your response.

Practice Mindful Presence

Anchor yourself in the present. Whether through journaling, breathwork, or quiet reflection, mindfulness allows clarity to replace chaos and intention to replace impulse.

Seek Supportive Connections

Surround yourself with people who reflect your strength back to you. Let encouragement and accountability fuel your growth.

Celebrate Your Wins

Acknowledge each success —big or small. Every step forward strengthens your belief in your own capability.

Visualize Success

See yourself succeeding before you do. Visualization activates motivation and aligns your mindset with your goals.

Learn and Adapt

Setbacks are teachers. Examine them, extract the lesson, and use it to refine your next move. Growth thrives in reflection, not regret.

Seek Professional Guidance if Needed

If old patterns persist, a therapist or life coach can help uncover hidden barriers and provide tools for sustainable change.

Each step you take to reclaim personal agency weakens the hold of victimhood. Over time, your life begins to reflect the confidence and courage that grow from intentional action.

Embracing Personal Empowerment
Transforming Awareness into Action

As we conclude this chapter on overcoming the loss of personal agency within a victim mindset, it's important to reflect on the journey of transformation we've explored. Recognizing how powerlessness breeds passivity and hesitation is the first step toward reclaiming control of your life.

Breaking free from these chains begins with understanding your own strengths and capacities. Empowerment grows when you see challenges not as barriers, but as opportunities for growth. This path toward greater agency calls for self-awareness, resilience, and the courage to confront limiting beliefs.

By taking ownership of your choices and approaching life with intention, you transcend the confines of victimhood and step into self-empowerment. May the insights from this chapter serve as your compass, guiding you toward a future where you actively shape your destiny and embrace the limitless potential within.

Passivity is another hallmark of victim mentality, where we may feel that life happens to us rather than believing we have the power to shape our own destinies. In this chapter, we explored how to overcome passivity by cultivating personal agency—the belief that you have control over your actions and their outcomes. By taking proactive steps, you can begin to transform your life from one of helplessness to one of empowerment.

As you reflect on these ideas, think about areas where you've been passive and how you can start taking control of your life.

Your Journey

"I am in control of my actions and my life's direction."

Reflect

In what areas of your life do you tend to drift rather than decide?

How might taking ownership of your choices shift your experience in these areas?

____

____

____

____

Discover

Recall on a situation where you chose silence or passivity over action.

How did that choice affect the outcome?

____

____

____

____

____

____

____

____

____

____

____

Transform

Identify one area where you want to be more proactive. Take one step today that says "I chose me".

Set a goal to replace passivity with conscious action in one area of your life this week.

Call to Action
Igniting Your Inner Power

Now, armed with insights and strategies, it's time to turn awareness into movement:

Reflect Intentionally: Identify moments when you've felt powerless. What beliefs kept you from acting?

Challenge the Narrative: Replace limiting thoughts with truth — you are capable of creating change.

Set Manageable Goals: Start small and build from there. Momentum grows with consistency.

Act Daily: Take one deliberate action each day that reinforces your sense of control.

Own Every Choice: Embrace the power of your choices. Even a decision to pause is still a decision — make it consciously.

Build Support: Surround yourself with those who believe in your potential.

Celebrate Growth: Recognize every effort. Confidence grows through acknowledgment.

Stay Present: Mindfulness keeps you grounded in choice and possibility.

Learn Gracefully: Let setbacks guide you not define you. Approach setbacks as opportunities for growth rather than reasons for retreat. Analyze challenges, extract lessons, and apply them to refine your approach.

Consider Professional Guidance: If the journey feels challenging, seek the guidance of a therapist or life coach. Professional support can offer valuable insights and strategies for overcoming mental barriers.

Each choice you make to act rather than wait is a declaration of empowerment. The path to personal empowerment is uniquely yours, and change is a gradual process. By actively engaging in these actions, you embark on a journey of self-discovery, resilience, and proactive living. This is how you move from drifting to directing, from surviving to creating — one conscious act of courage at a time.

Ignite your inner power, break free from the shackles of passivity, and step into a life where you are the conscious author of your narrative.

Shifting Perspectives

Breaking Free from the Grip of a Victim Mentality's Negative Outlook

Within the tangled web of a victim mentality lies a persistent thread that seems impossible to untwine — a deeply rooted negative outlook that colors how life is seen and experienced. Those caught in this pattern often find themselves trapped in a web of pessimism, where every challenge feels heavier and every setback overshadows possibility. Hope doesn't vanish; it simply hides behind the belief that life is working against them. Through this tinted lens, even moments of light are questioned, as the mind instinctively searches for what could go wrong instead of what could go right.

This habitual focus on the adverse casts a shadow over even the most promising moments. Challenges appear magnified, while successes fade beneath the weight of doubt. The ability to see opportunity shrinks as pessimism drowns out hope, reinforcing a cycle that feeds itself — the more one dwells on life's hardships, the less room there is to see potential.

Breaking free from the clutches of negativity requires conscious effort — a willingness to question automatic thoughts, shift focus toward the positive, and rebuild a mindset that sees possibility even in imperfection. By unweaving the web of pessimism, you begin to perceive a broader spectrum of life, one defined not by limitation but by potential and resilience.

Through the Shadows
David's Struggle with Negativity

David's story unfolds beneath the weight of a heavy cloak of victim mentality. For as long as David could remember, life felt like a long hallway lined with closed doors. He'd knock, wait, and when no one answered, he'd shrug and say, "Figures."

At work, a missed deadline or small mistake became proof he wasn't good enough. When his supervisor said, "You did well overall—just double-check those numbers next time," David heard only, *You failed again.* His thoughts had a way of turning whispers into thunder.

It wasn't just his job. Even at home, his girlfriend's quiet moments became signs she was losing interest. A canceled plan with a friend became confirmation that people didn't value him. His world was painted in grayscale — muted, heavy, and predictable.

Then came the afternoon that cracked everything open. David was sitting alone in his car after work, rain tapping against the windshield. He'd just been passed over for a project he wanted, and the words *"You're not ready yet"* echoed in his head like a verdict.

In frustration, he slammed his hand against the steering wheel. "Why does this always happen to me?" he muttered. But the question hung in the air, hollow — and suddenly, he heard it differently. *Does it really always happen to me… or do I just expect it to?*

That moment of honesty hit like a spotlight.

He realized that while life wasn't always fair, he had been feeding the very story that kept him stuck. His focus on what went wrong blinded him to what went right. He was the one keeping the hallway dark.

From that night forward, David made a quiet pact with himself: to find one thing — just one — that went well each day. Some mornings it was as small as catching a green light or finishing his coffee before it went cold. But slowly, those tiny sparks lit up the hallway.

He began surrounding himself with people who spoke hope into the conversation, who reminded him that optimism wasn't denial — it was direction.

The world hadn't changed — but his perception had.

David's story reminds us that freedom from negativity isn't about pretending everything's perfect. It's about noticing what *is* working, even in the midst of what isn't. Every time he chose gratitude over gloom, he loosened the chains that once bound him.

And as the shadows lifted, he discovered that joy had never left him. It was there, waiting, just beneath the dust of old beliefs — patient, persistent, and ready to shine again.

Transforming Perspectives
A Guide to Overcoming Negative Outlook

Self-Reflection

Notice when negativity colors your perception. What triggers it? Awareness is the first step toward change.

Challenge Negative Thoughts

Catch automatic reactions. Ask, *Is this thought true—or just familiar?* Replace assumptions with balanced, reality-based views.

Focus on the Positives

Acknowledge small victories and moments of joy. The mind expands in the direction of what it repeatedly notices.

Practice Gratitude

Write down three things you're grateful for each day. Gratitude shifts your inner dialogue from complaint to appreciation.

Stay Present

Mindfulness helps you step out of mental storms. Focus on what's happening now instead of what went wrong before.

Reframe Challenges

View obstacles as stepping stones, not dead ends. Each challenge reveals an opportunity to strengthen your resilience.

Use Positive Affirmations

Remind yourself daily of your strength and worth. Words repeated become beliefs — choose empowering ones.

Surround Yourself with Light

Engage with people and environments that lift you. Positivity is contagious; so is pessimism. Choose your energy wisely.

Set Realistic Goals

Break ambitions into smaller steps. Achievement builds momentum and confidence.

Practice Self-Compassion

Be gentle with yourself. Progress is rarely linear, and every setback is part of growth.

Learn from Setbacks

Treat challenges as feedback, not failure. Each one holds a lesson that refines your path forward.

Seek Support if Needed

Sometimes, the most courageous act is asking for help. Healing doesn't have to be a solo journey.

When you begin to apply these principles, you open the door to lasting change. Transformation isn't a single moment of awakening — it grows quietly, through intentional thought, patience, and practice.

Unshackling the Chains of Negativity

As we conclude this exploration of the profound link between a victim mentality and a negative outlook on life, we've delved into the intricate ways in which pessimism can cast a pervasive shadow on one's experiences. The struggle to recognize opportunities for positive change amid the fog of negativity is a poignant challenge faced by those navigating the complexities of a victim mindset. Yet, understanding this connection serves as a powerful catalyst for transformation. By acknowledging the impact of a negative outlook, individuals gain the insight needed to challenge and reshape their thought patterns.

As you move forward, remember that the journey towards a more positive perspective is a gradual process. Embrace the small victories, cultivate gratitude, and consciously shift your focus towards the possibilities that lie beyond the constraints of pessimism. In doing so, you unlock the potential for personal growth, resilience, and a more optimistic embrace of life's unfolding journey.

Perspective is everything. A negative outlook can keep us locked in a cycle of victim mentality, where we only see obstacles and limitations. By changing the way you view your circumstances, you can open up new possibilities for growth and success.

Take a moment to reflect on how your current perspective might be holding you back and consider how you can begin to see things differently.

Your Journey

"I choose to see possibilities where others see limitations."

Reflect

How has a negative outlook affected your life and relationships?

What could change if you shifted your perspective to focus on possibilities rather than limitations?

____

____

____

____

____

Discover

Write about a recent situation where you had a negative outlook.

How could a different perspective have changed the outcome of your emotional response?

____

____

____

____

____

____

____

____

____

____

____

____

____

Transform

Spend the next week practicing reframing. When a negative thought appears, counter it with a balanced or positive truth.

Note in your journal any shifts in your emotions, energy, or behavior.

Choose one area of your life where you struggle with negativity. How can you begin to see it through a different lens?

____

____

____

____

____

____

____

____

____

Call to Action
Cultivating Positivity and Resilience

Now it's time to put awareness into action:

Reflect: Identify moments when negativity shapes your outlook. What thoughts repeat most often?

Challenge: Replace those thoughts with balanced truths rooted in possibility.

Gratitude: Write down three things you appreciate today — no matter how small.

Connection: Spend time with those who lift your energy and challenge your pessimism.

Mindfulness: Pause throughout your day to breathe and reset your focus.

Visualize: Picture yourself succeeding; let that image guide your next action.

Celebrate: Acknowledge small wins — they are proof of progress.

Seek Support: If needed, talk to a professional who can help you reshape thought patterns.

Change doesn't happen overnight — and that's okay. Building positivity and resilience is a journey, not a race. It's about showing up for yourself, one small choice at a time, even on the days when it feels easier to slip back into old patterns.

Be patient with yourself. Every time you choose gratitude over frustration or hope over fear, you're planting seeds that will grow into strength and confidence. Those little moments matter — they add up, even when you don't notice it right away.

Celebrate your progress, no matter how small it seems. And when life throws challenges your way, try to see them as opportunities to learn and rise stronger. Over time, positivity becomes more than a mindset — it becomes your way of being.

With each intentional step, you're shaping a life that feels lighter, brighter, and more aligned with who you truly are. So, trust the process. Keep going. The more you nurture positivity, the more resilience will naturally take root in your life.

You're not just breaking free from negativity — you're stepping into a future where growth, peace, and possibility are waiting for you.

Embracing Growth
Breaking Through the Resistance to Feedback

In the framework of a victim mindset, resistance to feedback often becomes a quiet saboteur of growth. Constructive input can feel like criticism, reinforcing the belief that the world is against you. It protects the ego but imprisons the self, sealing off the very insight that could set you free.

When feedback is viewed as an attack, relationships suffer too. Collaboration turns defensive, and trust begins to erode. The turning point comes when you shift from hearing judgment to hearing opportunity. The moment you move from "They're criticizing me" to "They're helping me grow," the entire experience transforms. Feedback becomes less about fault and more about evolution.

This change takes conscious effort. When you find yourself reacting defensively to feedback, pause and ask why. Are you feeling vulnerable or threatened? Awareness disarms defensiveness, making space for curiosity and understanding.

As you learn to welcome feedback, new doors open. Connection deepens, teamwork strengthens, and resilience grows. You stop fearing mistakes because you see them for what they are — teachers. Every piece of feedback becomes a mirror, showing not what's wrong with you, but what's possible for you.

The Wall of Resistance
Emily's Battle with Feedback

Emily was known for her work ethic — always the first one in, the last one out. But beneath her determination was a quiet fear of not being good enough. The smallest critique could send her spiraling.

I remember her telling me about the day her manager called her in after a presentation. "It was good," he said, "but next time, try to slow down — let your ideas breathe."

That one comment undid her.

She smiled politely in the moment, but inside, a familiar fire rose. *Slow down?* she thought. *He has no idea how hard I worked on this.* By the time she got home, the story had grown — it wasn't feedback anymore; it was rejection. Proof, in her mind, that no matter what she did, she'd never measure up.

That night, she replayed the conversation again and again, each time layering on more resentment. It wasn't just her boss anymore — it was everyone. Her friends who offered advice. Her sister who tried to help. Even a kind suggestion from a coworker felt like a jab. The more she resisted, the thicker her wall grew.

But what Emily didn't realize was that the wall she built to protect herself was the same one keeping her stuck. It blocked growth, opportunity, and connection.

The shift came on an ordinary Tuesday. During a team meeting, her manager asked for her thoughts on a new project. She froze. For the first time, she saw the pattern — how her silence, her defensiveness, and her unwillingness to hear feedback were holding her back.

Later that night, she sat in her car in the quiet parking lot, tears rolling down her cheeks. "What if they're not against me?" she whispered to herself. "What if they're trying to help me?"

That was the crack in the wall.

From that moment, Emily decided to try something new — not perfection, just openness. The next time feedback came, she listened. She took notes. She asked questions. And to her surprise, the world didn't collapse. Her confidence didn't shrink — it grew.

The very thing she once feared became the thing that helped her evolve. Feedback stopped feeling like an attack and started feeling like a mirror — reflecting both her strengths and the places she could stretch.

Over time, her relationships deepened. Her performance improved. But more importantly, Emily stopped fighting the world. She began working *with* it.

Her story reminds us that resistance often hides fear — and that when we lower our defenses, we don't lose power. We gain wisdom. Feedback, when welcomed instead of feared, becomes the bridge between who we are and who we're becoming.

Transforming Resistance into Growth
The Feedback Integration Process

Before you can fully embrace feedback as a catalyst for growth, you must first understand your relationship with it. Every piece of feedback carries a choice: to resist it or to grow through it. The difference lies in perception. When you learn to listen without fear, feedback transforms from something that wounds into something that awakens. The steps below guide you through this shift — one reflection, one response, one act of courage at a time.

1. Acknowledge Resistance
Notice when defensiveness arises. Recognize how it affects your growth and your relationships. Awareness is the first step toward change.

2. Reframe Feedback
See feedback as guidance for your actions, not a judgment of your worth. Separate behavior from identity to evaluate input objectively.

3. Develop a Growth Mindset

Challenges are opportunities to expand your skills. Believe your abilities can evolve with effort, patience, and practice.

4. Practice Active Listening

Fully hear feedback before responding. Resist filtering it through fear or self-criticism — listen with curiosity.

5. Seek Clarity

Ask questions when feedback is unclear. Dialogue deepens understanding and uncovers insights you might otherwise miss.

6. Turn Insights into Action

Choose specific steps to implement suggestions. Transform awareness into tangible growth, and track progress along the way.

7. Express Gratitude

Acknowledge those offering feedback. Their input reflects an investment in your growth, not a critique of your character.

8. Build Your Support Network

Surround yourself with people who encourage reflection, challenge you constructively, and celebrate your progress.

Once you've learned to meet feedback with openness, the next step is turning awareness into action. Growth doesn't end with understanding — it begins when understanding becomes movement.

Embracing Growth Through feedback
Turning Awareness into Action

Growth doesn't happen in silence; it is shaped, stretched, and strengthened through feedback. Yet for someone caught in a victim mindset, feedback can feel threatening. Defensiveness rises, walls go up, and progress stalls.

But when you view feedback through a different lens, it transforms into a mirror reflecting not your flaws, but your potential. Each suggestion, each uncomfortable truth, can become a stepping stone toward a stronger, wiser version of yourself.

Breaking free from the resistance to feedback requires courage — the courage to listen without judgment, to stay open even when it stings, and to recognize that growth and discomfort often walk hand in hand.

Remember: Growth doesn't demand perfection; it asks only for openness. Welcoming feedback instead of fearing it invites transformation to take root — and that's where true progress begins.

Feedback can be challenging, especially when it touches on areas where we feel vulnerable. This chapter focused on overcoming resistance to feedback and using it as a tool for personal development. By welcoming constructive criticism, you can identify blind spots, make positive changes, and continue your journey of empowerment.

Now, think about how you respond to feedback and how you can use it to fuel your growth rather than seeing it as a threat.

Your Journey

"I welcome feedback as an opportunity for growth and self-improvement."

Reflect

How do you typically respond to feedback, especially when it challenges you?

What fears or insecurities arise when you receive feedback?

____

____

____

____

Discover

Recall a piece of feedback that once made you feel uncomfortable or defensive.

How do you view that feedback now? What has shifted in your understanding or response over time?

____

____

____

____

____

____

____

____

____

____

____

Transform

Think of one piece of feedback you've received recently. How can you use it as a tool for growth rather than as criticism? Reflect on one way you can apply it to strengthen yourself or your approach.

Choose one area where you'd like to grow and intentionally seek feedback. Approach it with openness and curiosity, viewing each insight as an opportunity to evolve.

____

____

____

____

____

____

____

____

____

____

Call to Action
Liberating Your Potential

You now stand at the threshold of transformation — where defensiveness ends and development begins. To break free from resistance and embrace growth, take these intentional steps:

Reflect: Identify patterns of defensiveness. What triggers resistance?

Challenge Perceptions: Reframe feedback as a tool for growth, not an attack.

Seek Input: Ask for guidance from colleagues, mentors, or loved ones with openness.

Separate Identity from Critique: Feedback evaluates actions, not your worth.

Adopt a Growth Mindset: Embrace learning through feedback and challenges.

Express Gratitude: Acknowledge the effort others invest in helping you improve.

Engage in Professional Development: Enhance skills in receiving and integrating feedback.

Foster Open Communication: Encourage honest dialogue and collaborative improvement.

When you choose to welcome feedback as a teacher, you embark on a journey of self-discovery and empowerment. Embrace feedback as a guide on the path to personal and professional growth. Liberating yourself from the chains of resistance opens doors to a future where constructive criticism becomes a beacon, illuminating the way towards a more resilient, skilled, and fulfilled version of yourself.

Each time you receive feedback with openness, you liberate a part of yourself once chained to fear. Feedback is not your enemy; it is your evolution speaking.

Overcoming Victim Mentality
Breaking the Cycle of Self-Pity

Self-pity can be a quiet but powerful force — the whisper that tells you life is unfair and that no matter what you do, the odds will always be stacked against you. In the landscape of a victim mentality, self-pity becomes both the storyteller and the script, casting you as the protagonist in a tragedy that never ends. It offers temporary comfort — a soothing justification for the pain — but that comfort comes at a steep cost.

Because self-pity doesn't heal; it traps.

It blinds us to moments of resilience and triumph, magnifying only what went wrong and who's to blame. It convinces us that we are powerless, quietly eroding the very sense of agency we need to move forward. Breaking free from this cycle requires a conscious shift — from "why me?" to "what now?" — replacing self-pity with awareness, gratitude, and personal responsibility.

When that shift happens, your story begins to change. You move from being life's casualty to being its creator. You begin to see that empowerment isn't about what happens to you, but about how you rise in response.

Trapped in the Tale
Alex's Struggle with Self-Pity

I'll never forget the day Alex called me after he didn't get the promotion. His voice was heavy, like someone carrying the weight of every missed chance in his life. "It doesn't matter what I do," he said. "They'll always find a reason to pass me over."

That moment was the spark — the start of a story he didn't realize he was writing about himself. One where life was always unfair, and he was always the one who lost.

At first, it was subtle. A joke that didn't land became proof no one respected him. A project that went sideways was "sabotaged." Even a friend canceling dinner was a sign that people just didn't care. It was as if every small disappointment joined the chorus of his inner critic, reinforcing the same old refrain: *"I can't win."*

The thing about self-pity is, it feels comforting at first. It gives you a story that explains the pain — and even justifies it. Alex started living inside that story. He replayed every unfair moment, polishing the details like a well-worn stone. He didn't see it, but he had built himself a cage — made of validation, lined with bitterness.

I watched the light fade from his ambition. He stopped pitching ideas at work. Stopped calling friends back. When I asked him what he wanted to do about it, he sighed and said, "What's the point? No one listens anyway."

It took hitting emotional rock bottom for Alex to realize that no one else was holding him there — he was gripping the bars himself. That realization cracked something open. Slowly, he began to question the story he'd been telling.

What if he wasn't powerless? What if setbacks weren't personal attacks but invitations to grow?

That shift didn't happen overnight, but day by day, Alex began to write a new story — one where challenges became lessons, and his voice, once filled with defeat, carried determination instead.

He started small: showing gratitude for the things that *did* go right, reaching out instead of retreating, taking ownership of his choices. Over time, that pattern rewired his perspective.

Alex's journey is proof that self-pity may comfort you for a moment, but empowerment sustains you for a lifetime. The story of unjust suffering became a story of resilience — and this time, Alex was no longer the victim. He was the author.

Breaking Free from Self-Pity
A Guide to Overcoming Victim Mentality

Breaking free from self-pity isn't about denying pain — it's about refusing to let it define you. When life feels unfair, it's easy to slip into the comfort of "why me?" But freedom begins the moment you realize that while you can't always control what happens to you, you can control what you do with it.

The following steps will guide you from self-pity to self-power — from seeing yourself as a victim of circumstance to becoming the author of your own recovery and resilience.

1. Awareness and Acknowledgment
Notice when self-pity takes hold. Recognize its effect on your thoughts, emotions, and behavior.

2. Challenge Distorted Narratives
Question the story you tell yourself. Are setbacks truly unfair, or is there another perspective that empowers you?

3. Practice Gratitude

Identify moments of strength, resilience, and joy. Gratitude shifts focus from what is lacking to what is present.

4. Cultivate Resilience

Reframe challenges as opportunities. Each setback holds lessons that strengthen your ability to navigate future difficulties.

5. Embrace Personal Agency

Focus on what you can control. Small, deliberate choices create meaningful change, even amid difficult circumstances.

6. Build Supportive Connections

Surround yourself with people who uplift and encourage you. Their perspectives can help break the cycle of self-pity.

7. Engage in Mindfulness

Observe thoughts without judgment. Mindfulness creates space to respond thoughtfully instead of reacting automatically.

8. Challenge Negative Thoughts in Real-Time

When self-pity arises, pause. Ask, *Is this thought factual or distorted?* Redirect attention toward constructive thinking.

9. Set Achievable Goals

Break larger objectives into manageable steps. Celebrate progress to reinforce confidence and capability.

10. Seek Professional Support if Needed

Sometimes self-pity hides deeper wounds. Therapy can offer tools to heal and rebuild emotional resilience.

Consistent practice of these principles fosters a mindset grounded in empowerment rather than helplessness. Transformation is gradual, but each conscious choice strengthens your resilience and expands your sense of possibility.

Transforming Perspective into Empowerment
Liberating Yourself from the Chains of Self-Pity

Self-pity can feel like a quiet companion—familiar, comforting even—but it slowly dims the light within us. It whispers that life is unfair, that we've been wronged, that the world owes us understanding. Yet, beneath that heaviness lies something deeper: a longing to rise, to reclaim our sense of power and possibility.

The truth is, self-pity traps us in a story that never moves forward. It feeds the belief that we are powerless, keeping us anchored to pain instead of progress. Freedom begins the moment we decide to shift that story—to see challenges not as punishments, but as invitations to grow stronger, wiser, and more self-aware.

Breaking this cycle takes courage. It means acknowledging the hurt without living in it, and choosing resilience over resignation. Each time we stand back up, we prove that our strength runs deeper than our suffering.

Let this be your reminder: the way out of self-pity isn't through blame or waiting for the world to change, it's through awakening your own agency. When you embrace responsibility for your path, you step into empowerment, and life begins to open in ways you never imagined.

It's easy to confuse self-pity with self-compassion, but they are not the same. Self-pity keeps you stuck; self-compassion helps you rise. One clings to suffering; the other transforms it.

By shifting our focus from what we lack to what we can do, we can begin to reclaim our power and move toward a brighter future.

As you reflect on this chapter, consider how self-pity might be affecting you and what steps you can take to overcome it.

Your Journey

"I am worthy of taking positive action, regardless of my circumstances."

Reflect

When do you find yourself slipping into self-pity, and how does it affect you?

What would it look like to respond to challenges from a place of empowerment instead of defeat?

____

____

____

____

Discover

Write about a time when self-pity held you back from taking action.

How might that story unfold differently if you approached it with strength, curiosity, or gratitude?

Transform

The next time you feel self-pity, take a moment to acknowledge the feeling, then redirect your focus to something positive or constructive.

Create a list of actions you can take when you notice self-pity creeping in. Use this list as a resource.

____

____

____

____

____

____

____

____

____

Breaking the Chains | Rosemarie Williams

____

____

Call to Action
Rediscovering Strength in Resilience

As you stand at the intersection of self-discovery, consider the following actionable steps to liberate yourself from the chains of self-pity:

• Reflect on patterns — notice when and where self-pity appears.

• Challenge the beliefs that feed it.

• Practice gratitude daily.

• Build resilience by viewing challenges as opportunities.

• Focus on personal agency — what can you do right now?

• Connect with people who see your potential.

• Engage in mindfulness to quiet distorted thoughts.

• Replace self-defeating narratives with empowering ones.

• Celebrate every small win.

• Seek professional help if old wounds keep resurfacing.

Liberating yourself from self-pity is not just about changing your mindset — it's about reclaiming your life. When you choose empowerment over helplessness, you don't just survive; you evolve.

Closing Message
Embracing Liberation

Dear Reader,

As we reach the final chapter of *Breaking the Chains: Understanding and Overcoming Victim Mentality*, I extend my heartfelt gratitude for embarking on this transformative journey. Together, we have navigated the intricate labyrinth of self-perception, resilience, and personal empowerment, unraveling the invisible chains that bind us to victimhood.

This book was written with the belief that within every individual lies the capacity for profound transformation. It is my sincere hope that the pages you've explored have served as a compass — guiding you toward a deeper understanding of the roots of victim mentality and offering practical strategies to break free from its grip.

As the author, my intention has been not only to illuminate the challenges of victimhood but to empower you to embrace the freedom and strength that come with liberation. Each insight, every personal story, and every exercise was crafted to foster awareness, encourage self-discovery, and inspire meaningful change.

Remember — breaking the chains is not a one-time event; it is a continual process of awareness, resilience, and conscious choice. As you close this book, carry with you the understanding that your mindset shapes your reality and that the power to reclaim your life has always been within you.

As we come to the end of this journey, it's time to embrace the liberation that comes from breaking free from victim mentality. This closing chapter is your call to action — an invitation to live what you've learned. By embracing your inherent power and taking full responsibility for your own happiness, you can create a future defined by strength, resilience, and infinite possibility.

Let this be your moment of renewal — to reflect on the path you've walked, the chains you've broken, and the courage you've discovered within yourself. Step forward with an open heart and an unshakable belief in your ability to shape your destiny.

With gratitude and unwavering belief in your journey,

Rosemarie

Let's reflect on the journey you've taken through this book and commit to living a life of empowerment and liberation.

Your Journey

"I am free to create a life of empowerment, growth, and endless possibilities."

Reflect

What does liberation from a victim mentality look like for you?

How will you continue to cultivate empowerment and personal agency in your life?

____

____

____

____

____

____

____

Discover

Take a moment to reflect on the journey you've taken through this book, the challenges faced, the truths uncovered, and the growth that's unfolded along the way.

What insights or transformations stand out to you the most? How have they begun to shape the way you see yourself and your life?

Transform

Write a commitment to yourself about how you will continue to embrace liberation and reject victim mentality.

Identify one area of your life where you will actively apply the lessons learned in this book moving forward.

Freedom is not the absence of challenge, but the presence of courage. You have walked through awareness, truth, and transformation and emerged stronger.

Carry forward the light you've uncovered within yourself. Let it guide your choices, shape your voice, and illuminate your path.

You are no longer bound by the stories of the past.
You are the author of your own evolution —unbroken, unchained, and free.

Continue the Journey

Your story doesn't end here, it's just beginning. *Breaking the Chains* was created to spark awareness, inspire growth, and encourage transformation, but the deeper work often unfolds through shared conversation and connection.

If you're looking to bring these insights to your community, organization, or audience, Rosemarie Williams is available for:

Speaking Engagements

Invite Rosemarie to speak at conferences, retreats, or events where audiences seek personal growth, leadership development, or emotional empowerment. Her engaging style weaves storytelling, insight, and practical tools that help people shift from limitation to possibility.

Guest Podcast Appearances

Rosemarie brings warmth, clarity, and authentic conversation to podcast audiences. She speaks openly about transformation, self-leadership, silent communication, and the power of awareness in breaking free from self-imposed limitations.

Workshops & Interactive Sessions

For groups, organizations, or teams ready to dig deeper, Rosemarie offers customized workshops designed to inspire self-awareness, communication mastery, and personal empowerment. Participants walk away with actionable tools to break through barriers and lead from within.

To inquire about availability or collaboration, contact Rosemarie at: **rosemariespage@outlook.com**

Together, we can help others step into awareness, growth, and freedom—one conversation at a time.

Amazon.com: Rosemarie Williams: books, biography, latest update